Simple(r) Social Media

What You Actually Need to Know, Whether You're

Just Starting or Overseeing Someone Else

JeremyLesniak Consulting

by Jeremy Lesniak

Last Updated May 10, 2021

Contents

Introduction 5
    What is This Guide and Who is it for? 5
    How is This Guide Different from Others? 5
    Why Should You Listen to Me? 5
    Social Media is Constantly Changing 6
    What Social Media is and is Not 6
    How to Define Social Media Success 6

Building a Social Media Strategy 9
    What Social Media Sites Should I Care About? 9
    Does Every Business Need Social Media? 9
    What About New Social Media Sites? 10
    Professional vs Personal Accounts 10

The Most Important Social Media Websites 11

Creating Social Media Content 13
    Where to Get the Best Elements 13
        Stock Photography 13
        Quotes 13
        Post Ideas 14
    Experimentation 14
    Reposting Content from Others 14
    Branding Your Content 15
    Social Media Strategy Builder 15
        Example Social Media Strategy Builder 16
    Content Does Not Have to be Perfect 18
    Types of Content 18

- Jokes 18
- Memes 18
- Photos 18
- Videos 18
- Quotes 19
- History 19
- Surveys/Polls 19
- Discussion Questions 19
- Expert Commentary 19
- Cool Stuff 19
- Reposts from Other Accounts 19
- Self-Promotional/Sales/New Products/Announcements 19
- What Not to Post 20
- Attracting Attention 21
  - Getting Others to Repost Your Content 21
  - Digging out of The Hole 21
  - Catering to Your Audience 22
  - Going Viral 23
  - Engaging with your Audience 23
  - Inviting People to Follow Your Brand 23
  - Buying Followers 24
  - Promoting Your Business from your Personal Account 24
  - Handling Criticism 24
- Growth Considerations 26
  - When to Outsource 26
  - Reporting 26

Scheduling Tools 28
Following Experts 29
Social Media in One Hour Per Week 30
Final Thoughts 31
Blank Social Media Strategy Builder 32

Introduction

What is This Guide and Who is it for?

This guide is for busy professionals and executives who are interested in staying aware of the current social media landscape so they can make better decisions. It is also for individuals who are new to social media and/or those responsible for handling an organization's social media presence as a smaller piece of their responsibilities.

How is This Guide Different from Others?

I do not pretend that there aren't other books and courses that tackle this subject. However, in every case that I have seen, these other options make things overly complicated, or are targeted at those who are building a social media agency or are otherwise handling social media as their primary job function.

These other options are trying to get you to buy something expensive. This book, however, is meant to be a completely standalone product.

Why Should You Listen to Me?

If you have prior experience with social media or have read information from others, some of what I present may be contradictory. Why should you listen to me in these cases, or even at all?

I have been involved in social media from the early days. But that, on its own, does not qualify me. Currently, I oversee social media for my own organizations, as well as for a number of my clients. I do not have time to spend hours crafting the perfect social media post, nor do I think that is wise in most cases.

I simply see social media as a component of a larger marketing landscape and understand when and how to utilize it to further the goals of my organizations or my clients.

To say it another way, I do not have time for BS, and this guide is built on that principle. I will tell you what you need to know, and nothing more. It is direct, timely, and succinct.

Social Media is Constantly Changing

It is important to know that the social media landscape changes, sometimes rapidly. If you have purchased this, it has been updated recently. I promise to maintain this book in such a way that it remains useful to those who read it.

While the principles that I will review are unlikely to change rapidly, they may. The specifics of what platforms to use and how to use them, however, are likely to change quickly.

What Social Media is and is Not

Social media is not, by itself, going to revolutionize your business or bring you substantial new customers or add tons of money to your bottom line. While there are examples of companies and individuals who have capitalized on social media to great advantage, they are the exception, not the rule.

Even organizations that do a wonderful job of social media do not always see a great benefit from it. Thus, why does it even matter?

It matters because, just like having a website or a phone number or a physical address, the ownership and periodic usage of social media accounts is an important signal to your existing and potential customers. Without social media, not only do you seem disengaged from your customer base, but you may leave an opportunity for your competition to gain awareness and following from even your best customers.

Please know that throughout this book, I will use terms like customer and client, or business and organization, interchangeably.

How to Define Social Media Success

Have I or my clients seen success from social media? Absolutely. But let's talk about what success with social media means.

As with any marketing endeavor, the investment into social media should lead to profit, either directly or indirectly. Hiring a full-time employee or contracting out social media, at great expense, when it is not returning benefit, is a loss. There is no other way to say it.

Thus, when I evaluate a successful social media campaign, I am not simply looking at the metrics that social media platforms and other consultants suggest as all-important. The number of follows, likes, and comments are relevant, but they are only relevant as an intermediate Step 2 customer acquisition, retention, or sale.

This is an important concept because it means that you can adjust the number of resources that you put into your social media based on the results you are receiving. There is a point of diminishing return, no matter the organization. Just because posting three times a week is successful does not mean that posting six times a week will make you twice as successful.

When I think about what success has looked like for my companies or my clients, it has surfaced in a few different ways:

- Client retention
- Client acquisition
- Increased purchase/order value

Concerning client retention, social media can be a great way to tell the story of your brand and help your existing customers feel positive about engaging with you. We will cover the specifics of that later, but in short, it is about putting a face on your company, so people do not feel like they are dealing with a faceless brand.

When we talk about client acquisition, it is similar, but leverage is the principle of social proof - which happens as your existing clients like, comment, and share your material from social media - and makes a potential customer that much more likely to give you a try.

Increased order value (whether it is service or product does not matter) comes from the comfort that social media can build with an existing or new customer.

Because they are more comfortable, they are more likely to take a bigger risk when purchasing with you. Think about it, your loyal customers typically spend more money with you than a new customer.

Building a Social Media Strategy

What Social Media Sites Should I Care About?

There are a lot of social media sites out there these days. Some would suggest that you need to be active on all of them and put substantial resources behind every effort. That is simply not true.

Most social media sites are not worth your time. If you have any background in retail, you are likely familiar with the 80/20 rule. It applies just as well here, in that most social media websites can be all but ignored and most of your attention should go to the best few.

Below you will find a list of the most important social media sites currently, as well as some general demographic information and the size of the platform. I have prioritized these based on the general recommendations I would make to a client. However, it is important to know that different businesses will have different marketing needs, so the priorities for your business may be slightly different.

I suggest that every business secure the account or username for their brand from every social media platform. That is a one-time action and is a defense against a competitor or a similar brand taking your name. You do not have to use it, but you should secure it.

Does Every Business Need Social Media?

Are there organizations that do not need social media? No. However, the usage of social media for some organizations may be quite minimal. In these cases, I find that the organizations needing little social media are those that provide commodity services to businesses. As an example, FedEx does not need to do much with social media to maintain its visibility. Of course, they have accounts, but if you look at the metrics of the number of people who engage with their posts, it's quite small.

Why? Because when people utilize social media, most of the time they are doing so as individuals. Even if you go on Facebook while you are at work, you are doing so as an individual, rather than a representative of the company.

What About New Social Media Sites?

New social media websites pop up all the time. How do you know if they are worthwhile? By following a simple formula. When you learn of a new account, you should secure the relevant account name or username for your company. Then, assuming it does not take too long to do so, make a test post. Then, see what happens.

Most of the time, nothing will happen, because no one is using it yet. Are there circumstances where investing time into an unproven platform makes sense? Yes. But please remember the intended audience and goal of my writing. I am simply trying to give you an easy path forward for social media.

Professional vs Personal Accounts

Some platforms offer the ability to distinguish between a personal account and a business or professional account. It is important that if this option is given, that you follow it appropriately. There may be consequences to doing this improperly, especially if the social media platform is large enough to have the resources to care.

For example, in the early days of Facebook, companies would sign up as individuals. Then, Facebook rolled out several options for businesses to have their own pages, but those pages needed to be managed by personal accounts. Some ignored this advice and found that the logins that they were using, which had their business name on them, were shut down for violating terms of service. Like it or not, you must follow the rules as best you can, or else you may suffer consequences.

The Most Important Social Media Websites

I initially started this section by researching the number of users, monthly traffic, etc. What I found was that the numbers were all over the place, so I am leaving those out. What I am presenting is a basic priority list for a company, regardless of what they do. Keep in mind, that does not mean you should consider this appropriate for your brand. Instead of charging ahead and building a strategy with any or all of these, in the same order as I have laid them out, you should spend a bit of time researching what others in your industry are doing.

In general, if your competitors are somewhere, you should be there, too. But if there is somewhere they are not, and it lines up with the general guidance I provide below, you might consider making that site your priority.

- Facebook
    - The 800-pound gorilla of the space. It is rare for me to craft a social media strategy that does not position Facebook as the top priority. It's a good way to bring in new customers because of the scale and diversity of users.
- Instagram
    - Owned and run by Facebook, with lots of integration between the management tools of the two, Instagram is best for maintaining existing client relationships rather than discovery.
- YouTube
    - If you have the means to produce videos for YouTube, or you have videos that you already produce that can go here, it makes sense. YouTube is the second largest search engine, behind Google, and has a lot of opportunity to deepen relationships with clients and prospects who are looking for experts on particular subjects.
- LinkedIn
    - If you operate a business that primarily does business with other organizations, rather than individuals, LinkedIn is critical.

> For consumer-facing businesses, this is far less important and can be considered as an occasional place to post.
- Twitter
  - Some companies do very well on Twitter. Most do not. I have found it is the worst platform for most of my clients in terms of value. However, it still has the perception of being a top platform and for that reason, it should not be ignored. In other words, it will strike some clients as odd if you do not have a presence here.
- Pinterest
  - Pinterest either does very well or very poorly for businesses. I have found it to be a worthwhile investment for most businesses that produce original content or products. It does not take a lot of time to manage.
- TikTok
  - There is a tremendous opportunity on TikTok right now, but it is hard to say how much of that opportunity is translating to clientele and revenue. If you serve a broad geographic area (rather than a local one), and your target audience includes a large portion of under 30-year-olds, TikTok is worth consideration.
- Snapchat
  - It is unlikely that, if you are reading this guide, Snapchat will be relevant for your brand. There are use cases for it, but they are specific and it's generally not going to be a top-3 platform for many organizations.

Creating Social Media Content

Where to Get the Best Elements

Even in circumstances where you are creating all your posts, which is rare, you are still going to need to borrow elements from others. It is unlikely you have a massive library of original photos that cover all circumstances, nor is it even possible that every quote you want to use comes from your organization. You are going to need to look elsewhere, but the upside is that it saves you time.

Stock Photography

Most social media posts are going to contain a photo, so having access to good photos is an important part of crafting good social media. The following websites allow you to download and use any photo from their site for free. While the sites suggest that you offer attribution to the person that took the photo, it is not required.

- Unsplash.com
- StockSnap.io
- Pexels.com
- Reshot.com
- Pixabay.com

Quotes

There are many websites out there dedicated to quotes, but I find that I frequently just search for them on Google. If I am looking for a quote about enjoying the weather, for example, I will just search for *quotes about enjoying the weather*. Something is bound to come up, and there is no need to worry about licensing here. Just make sure that you get the quote right, and you attribute the quote to the person who said it.

If you are looking for or posting something controversial as a quote, I strongly urge you to do a bit of research to make sure the person being attributed actually said it.

Post Ideas

There are many ways to post something on social media. The sheer number of ideas of what you could post goes far beyond what I could write here. Usually, if someone is looking for ideas, I find that they are thinking too hard about this. Do not try to reinvent the wheel, and don't be afraid of seeming derivative. After all, social media is, to a certain degree, all about following the crowd.

If you are stuck for ideas, look at what your competition is posting and see if there is something that you can make better.

I have a saying: dogs, kids, and pretty people rule the Internet. If you look at what does best on social media, you will find that, quite often, one of those three elements is included.

Experimentation

I suggest following what I call the 15% rule when creating content. You can probably follow this rule for just about anything in business.

When you set out to create some content, 85% should be stuff that you know will be well received. If you are constantly looking at what you have posted in the past, and what has done reasonably well, this is just producing more of the same. You might even repost some of your content occasionally.

The remaining 15% should be somewhat experimental. It does not mean that you try completely ridiculous things, but things that are slightly different from what you have done before, posts that you aren't quite sure if they will do as well, or better, than what you have been posting.

Then, you evaluate the results and repeat the process. Over time, with this experimentation, you ultimately build a better understanding of what your customers will want to see, and you can better provide that to them.

Reposting Content from Others

Some might think that posting content from others in your industry is subservient to their brand. When, in fact, it shows that you are paying attention to what is going on and further positions your brand as being authoritative. You should provide a mix of posting content from brands that are larger than yours, as well as smaller than yours. Be sure not to edit or alter the post unless that is the entire purpose, say for humorous reasons. Always provide credit and, if the platform allows, tag or otherwise make a direct reference to the account from which it came.

I would discourage you from reposting others' content as anything more than 5% of what you post on social media.

Branding Your Content

Any original social media post you put up should have your logo on the accompanying photo, if applicable. If you are sharing someone else's post, do not do that, ever. If you have a complex logo or multiple logos, you want to do something quite simple and something that is only one or two colors. The logo on the image should be small and not detract from what you are posting, but simply reminds people that you made this. It can also be useful if someone saves your content and reposts it without giving you credit.

Social Media Strategy Builder

On the following page is an example of a document that I use to layout strategy for my businesses and my clients. You will notice that it is simple, and the entire purpose is to get you to think of things from an 800-foot view. You can always fill in details as you move forward later, but it's important to think about the macro perspective of a social media strategy.

While the following example does contain some specifics of an example organization, that does not mean that you should do exactly what is here. I can all but guarantee that what I have included here would not be ideal for you and your organization.

You should take this with a grain of salt, and layout your strategy to start. I have included a blank version of this document as the final page if you would like to print it.

Example Social Media Strategy Builder

Example Business: Bob's Plumbing & Heating

Monthly Budget: 12 hrs./month, content in batches every 2 weeks

Weekly Posts per platform

- Instagram - 5
- Facebook - 5
- Pinterest – none yet
- YouTube – none yet
- Twitter – 5
- LinkedIn – None yet

Notes: Post the same content on all 3 accounts, though not necessarily at the same time or in the same order.

Percentage of Posts Per Category (must = 100)

- Jokes - 5
- Memes - 25
- Photos – 20
- Videos – 0
- Quotes – 20
- History - 10
- Survey - 0
- Discussion Question – 0
- Expert Commentary - 5
- Cool Stuff - 5
- Self-Promotional/Sales/New Products/Announcements – 10

- New vs Reposted (must = 100%)
    - 95% New
    - 5% Reposted

- List of Other Accounts to Share From
  - https://www.bigrentz.com/blog/very-not-boring-history-plumbing
  - https://plumbingdynamicsdallas.com/15-interesting-plumbing-facts-and-tips/

- Percentage of shares from other accounts
  - 5%
- Should original graphics be watermarked?
  - Yes, with logo.

Content Does Not Have to be Perfect

There are times when things need to be perfect, and times when they do not. In most cases, social media does not need to be perfect. It is usually far better to have three or four imperfect posts rather than one perfect post that would take just as long to create.

We are also in this interesting time where individuals and brands have been so devoid of authenticity, that sometimes the imperfect posts are deemed more authentic and thus received better by the social media following. While I do not encourage intentional spelling errors or typographic mistakes, do not throw the baby out with the bathwater if you find one after you post something.

Types of Content

It is possible that a particular post could fit into several categories, and that is OK. There are no hard and fast rules here beyond the others that we have outlined. If you have a post that is both funny and historical, put it in whichever category you have a tougher time filling.

Jokes

Jokes as a category can be broad and do not have to be of the knock-knock variety. It could just be something funny and could be text, an image, video, etc., even a humorous meme.

Memes

Memes are images with photos on them and are usually saved and reposted. They can be humorous or serious, political, or personal.

Photos

If it is a photo, it's a photo.

Videos

Different platforms offer certain limitations on sharing a video. For example, Facebook seems to prefer if you post a video directly to the platform rather than sharing it from YouTube. Overall, though, videos are straightforward. You may find that videos with embedded captions do better than those without, as many people use social media without headphones or speakers while they are working.

Quotes
Try to focus on quotes that your audience will recognize.

History
Everyone likes historical facts and stories if they are presented the right way.

Surveys/Polls
Best accomplished with a tool like Survey Monkey or a built-in tool like the one Facebook uses. Unless you have thousands of followers, these do not generally do well.

Discussion Questions
Similar to a survey, but instead of taking a formal survey, you simply pose a question to the followers and invite conversation. Be cautious of the subjects and make sure you have either an engaged audience or thousands of followers for maximum impact.

Expert Commentary
This involves sharing or posting content from another account and then offering feedback on it. This is an underutilized form of content as it positions your brand as being authoritative. Be careful of critical commentary, especially if you are critiquing a smaller player in the industry.

Cool Stuff
This is a catch-all because sometimes you end up with stuff that just does not quite fit well elsewhere.

Reposts from Other Accounts
Straightforward – sharing or reposting content from another account, generally without saving it first. Most platforms give you a way to do this easily.

Self-Promotional/Sales/New Products/Announcements
This is the most difficult category for an organization, especially when that organization does not put many resources into social media. The temptation is

to turn everything into an appeal for doing business. But keep in mind, this is *social* media – would that work in real life? If you walk into a store and three seconds after you pass the doorway, an employee asks you if they can help you, how do you respond? Take that same attitude to social media and make your promotional posts infrequent AND give them value of their own.

What do I mean? If you post about a sale, add in something that gives the viewer value even if they do not participate. That could be a quote, a tip on using a product, or something else. Help them feel good about everything you post, even your sales, and the posts will be seen by more people.

What Not to Post

Unless your organization is a political non-profit, I would strongly urge you to stay away from anything political or overly controversial. It is easy to allow our political views to creep into our business decisions, but the ramifications of this can be huge.

Also, be careful of being critical of any individual or organization, especially if your followers will perceive them as being smaller than you. Posting criticism of a large corporation may be received in the way you intend it, but if you are a large corporation and you post something about a smaller organization, that is probably going to go over poorly.

If I am unsure whether I should post something because it will be deemed as controversial or inflammatory, I try to focus on whether it will be received positively or not. Do I want people following my organization to associate negative feelings with what I do? Absolutely not. There is enough negativity in the world, and it takes a lot of nuance and planning to post critical or negative things on social media. If you are reading this guide, you probably do not want to invest the time in doing that well.

Attracting Attention

Getting Others to Repost Your Content

One of the best ways to gain attention across social media is to create content that is appealing to others in such a way that they will repost what you have made. There are several ways to do this.

One of the easiest ways is to create the type of content that your audience is posting personally. For example, if your audience contains a large percentage of people who watch basketball, then posting a quote from a prominent basketball player embedded into an image of that player is likely to attract some attention.

If you work backward from what it is your audience is posting personally, you will have a better shot at attracting their attention and getting them to redistribute what you have produced.

Digging out of The Hole

I have often had new clients come to me and tell me that they have recently put effort into their social media only to find it has yielded little to no result. When I dig into what they have been posting, they typically left their social media to be ignored for quite some time or posted a large percentage of self-promotional items. This creates a situation that I call needing to dig yourself out of the hole.

Consider social media platforms and their job. They are trying to show their users the things that they most want to see at any given time. If it is a platform where people only follow a few people or brands, that is not a big deal. But most platforms have grown to the scope where users are following hundreds or even thousands of people and brands. Even if a small percentage of those that they follow produced content daily, it is impossible to see all of it.

This leads the platform to make decisions as to what to show you. These platforms utilize an algorithm that is extraordinarily complex and not entirely known for making these decisions. But there is something that we can say about how it works.

This algorithm uses a few pieces of information that are obvious: how often the user has engaged with content of that type, as well as how often other users have engaged with content of that type.

If your brand puts out nothing but promotional material on social media, and nobody likes it or comments on it, that is a signal to the platform that this content from this brand is not of value, meaning that the next time you put up content of any kind, it is less likely to be seen.

This situation can be incredibly frustrating for organizations that are trying to dig out of the hole and do not have a lot of resources to invest in social media. In these cases, I suggest you reduce the quality of the posts that you were putting up, increase the frequency, and fall back to a handful of types of posts that are likely to receive engagement:

- children
- animals
- motivational quotes
- industry humor
- and, if it lines up with your brand, sex appeal

Over time, these posts are going to be seen and start to create some momentum. Through these times, you can also utilize your personal accounts as well as the accounts of friends, family, and staff, to create some engagement. If a bunch of people think something is worthwhile, social media platforms are likely to show it to a bunch of other people.

Catering to Your Audience

The better you know your audience, which should be your customer base and potential customers, the easier it is to create content that is relevant to them. This does not mean you should get narrowly focused and only show things that are exactly what you do. If you sell hiking equipment, you should not only have photos of mountain tops and quotes from hikers or famous explorers. You should, instead, think about what is important to people who enjoy hiking and post things that will appeal to them.

For example, people who hike generally enjoy the outdoors and value health and fitness. They tend to care about the environment and often own dogs that they bring on their hikes. If you sell equipment for hiking, there might be a temptation to post about the latest gear or your current sale, but what about posting information on trail conditions or celebrating the accomplishments of someone who completed something challenging?

Going Viral

Every organization wants to see something that they post go viral. If you are unfamiliar with the term, a viral post gets distributed among a social media platform at a far higher rate than normal. For example, if you typically get 100 likes on a post, a viral post might be 10,000.

A lot of marketing agencies have invested a lot of time to try and find how to make things go viral. The short answer to how to do this is that there is no answer. Virality is a simple result of a complex equation. There is no gaming it. Instead of trying to worry about going viral, just focus on making great content for your audience. Attempts to go viral are like buying a lottery ticket. It is great if it works out, but it's statistically unlikely and, in most cases, a waste.

Engaging with your Audience

One of the best ways to build a social media following is to show the community of users that you are giving back and engaging with others. If someone comments on your post, reply or at the very least like their comment. This will show people that real individuals are managing the account. Remember, one of the best uses of social media is to put a personality or a face to your brand.

Inviting People to Follow Your Brand

On some platforms, you can invite people to follow you or become friends with your brand. Even if they are not part of your target customer demographic, this can be an important step early on. If your brand has few followers, it can be hard to get more followers, because the social proof suggests that your brand is not worth following. The more people that follow your brand, the more we can shift that social proof in the other direction and the platform will suggest that people follow you.

Buying Followers

Some third-party businesses will sell you followers, likes, and comments. It can be tempting to purchase these, especially when you are starting, but in most situations, it is a waste of money and can even set you back if the social media platform determines that your followers were fake. Yes, they are looking for that and trying to stop it.

Promoting Your Business from your Personal Account

If you have a personal account on a platform and a separate business or professional account or page, it can be beneficial to share the professional posts on your personal page. It is not something that you should do frequently, but occasionally it is probably a good thing, especially if you own the company. After all, your friends and family probably want to know what is going on with what you do, and it could create additional followers or engagement.

Handling Criticism

Inevitably, someone will criticize something that you post. It is important to avoid content that you know will receive criticism if possible, but we live in a world where people are looking for things to be upset about.

Advice on how to handle this differs and the specifics of what to do can vary dramatically based on the circumstances. However, here are a few guidelines.

If you made a substantial error and posted something that you see in hindsight should have never been posted, remove it and make a new post that explains what happened and the corrective action you have taken.

If you made a small error, leave the post up and either edit or comment on it that you made an error and are thankful that people pointed it out.

If you do not think that you have made an error, how you respond to the criticism depends on how that criticism was made. If it is over the top, offensive, or angry, I would suggest deleting it and blocking the user. If it was made more respectfully, engaging with that individual and trying to find out what has upset them may be relevant.

Here are a couple of things to keep in mind when responding to criticism. First, try to use the same rules of decorum that you would in a personal conversation. If someone is yelling at you and swearing at you, you are unlikely to stand and receive that. You would probably just hang up the phone or walk away. Second, remember the old saying, "never argue with a fool, people at a distance cannot tell who is who."

Often, the right action is that you should engage with them, but do not be afraid to simply delete their comment if it is warranted. It will upset them, but in most cases, the overly critical people are not your customers, anyway.

Growth Considerations

When to Outsource

I have mentioned a couple of times that I have clients for whom I manage social media. This might make you think that I am going to try to sell you hard to use my services or those of someone similar. That is not the case.

In fact, for most organizations, outsourcing social media is a bad move. I have had clients surprised that the time involved in working with my firm is almost as much as them doing their social media themselves. The difference is, we can do it better and at greater volume. The tradeoff is that it costs money.

So, when do you outsource? If your social media is yielding results, yet you suspect there is the opportunity for even better results, but you lack the time or knowledge to take the next step, that is the point at which to enlist an expert.

How to evaluate a social media agency and what to spend is outside the scope of this book. The rules on success, are the same. If you are making money, directly or indirectly, because of your social media, then it is worth the investment. If you are spending $1,000 a month on social media, and you see no visible uptick in revenue or profit, nor are the engagement numbers from the social media efforts moving in the right direction, it is time to find a new agency.

Reporting

I have found that the easiest way for me to oversee my client's social media is to make sure that my staff is tracking the right numbers at the right frequency. Like anything in business, if you cannot evaluate it, you can't change it.

For any of the platforms that I am managing, I look at the number of people following the brand, their engagement, whether it be likes or comments, as well as what social media content has done well and not done well over time. I find that tracking this information in a spreadsheet regularly is the easiest way to show trends. If you are a larger brand, and hyper-focused on social media, you might track these numbers daily. For most organizations, tracking every two weeks or even once a month is adequate.

Within that tracking, identifying which posts did the best and did the worst is important. Being able to look at what continually does well, and understanding why, is critical to growing your social media and presenting more of what your audience wants.

I have found that with most established organizations, looking at trends on a 90-day cycle makes the most sense. If you were to delegate social media to a staff member, you might look at how those numbers did quarterly.

Scheduling Tools

Some tools make social media simpler. One of the most important is a scheduling tool. The premise is simple: by having an account with a third-party scheduling tool, you can connect your social media accounts to that tool and then create your content there. This allows you to post the same content on multiple platforms if that makes sense for you. It also means that you can create a bunch of content ahead of time and schedule it for later release.

In the effort to be efficient with social media, this is critical.

At this time, if you do not already have a social media scheduling tool, I would suggest Buffer. I receive no benefit from you using them, or anyone else. I have simply found it to be a good place for people to start. **Bufferapp.com**

If the only social media platform you are using is Facebook, there is an integrated scheduling tool that you can use.

Following Experts

Social media does not make up a large portion of my business or time. However, it is an important tool and I pay attention to others and to what they say about social media. I think it is important to identify those that are worth following to see how these platforms are being used so that you can learn from them.

Currently, I am a fan of Gary Vaynerchuk, Jason Capital, Grant Cardone, and Tony Robbins when it comes to social media. In each case, these individuals do not manage their social media directly, but rather have a team of people doing so. By watching these successful individuals and what they are doing, you may not find things that you can replicate. However, if you look at the types of things they are doing, you can pull out concepts that may apply to your organization.

You should also be paying attention to your direct competitors. What are they doing that you could be doing? Specifically, what are they doing that you could do even better?

Social Media in One Hour Per Week

When I talk to people about social media, they tell me that they do not have time to do it. Maybe you don't have time to do it comprehensively, but you have time to do it. If I was responsible for a brand and had to manage the social media but I could only get an hour a week to do so, here is what I would do.

I would pick a single social media platform that I could post to. It should be the one that either has, or is most likely to have, my target customers. I would look to see what my competitors are doing and try to find the platform that my customers are on, but my competitors are ignoring. For most brands, that is currently Instagram.

I would get a tool, like Buffer, and I would make several simple posts based on the following breakdown:

3 posts per week:

- 2 motivational quotes from someone famous over a piece of stock photography
- 1 picture of a pet or child doing something funny.

Once I get the hang of that…

- Every other week I would use one photo of a staff person or product with text accompaniment of something positive. "Have a good weekend" or similar.
- Once a month I would post something that had to do with a sale, product feature, new product, etc.
- (The two above would be part of the 3 posts per week.)
- Once a week I would like/reply to any of the comments people made on your posts

Final Thoughts

Social media is not simple, but it doesn't have to be overly complicated. Do not listen to the media telling you that everything you do has to be presented on your social media pages and that this needs to comprise such a large part of your day or your business efforts.

Instead of seeing social media as a necessity, try to find the opportunity in it. If the opportunity is small, the investment should be small. If the opportunity is large, it might warrant a larger investment. Do not be afraid to experiment, and don't be afraid to recognize that something didn't work. As with anything else in your business, learn what you can and move on.

If you would like to get in touch with me for any reason,
jeremy@jeremylesniak.com

Thanks for reading!
~jeremy

Blank Social Media Strategy Builder

<u>Monthly Budget</u>: hrs./month, content in batches every # of weeks

How Frequently Should Content Be Produced:

<u>Weekly Posts per platform</u>

- Instagram
- Facebook
- Pinterest
- YouTube
- Twitter
- LinkedIn

Should content be repeated across accounts or original?

<u>Percentage of Posts Per Category (must = 100)</u>

- Jokes
- Memes
- Photos
- Videos –
- Quotes –
- History -
- Survey -
- Discussion Question –
- Expert Commentary
- Cool Stuff
- Reposts from Other Accounts -
- Self-Promotional / Sales / New Products / Announcements -

- New vs Reposted (must = 100%)
    - % New
    - % Reposted
- List of Other Accounts to Share From
    -
- The required percentage of original graphics (for posts that are not reposts, of course)
    -
- Percentage of shares from other accounts
    -
- Should original graphics be watermarked?

www.ingramcontent.com/pod-product-compliance
Lightning Source LLC
Chambersburg PA
CBHW070909220526
45466CB00005B/2181